ABC LETTER TRACING
for preschoolers

A Fun Book to Practice Writing for Kids Ages 3-5

We create our books with love and great care.

Yet mistakes can always happen. For any issues with your book, such as faulty binding, printing errors, or something else, please do not hesitate to contact us at: **eduplayhub@gmail.com**
We will make sure you get a replacement copy immediately.

For any suggestions or questions regarding our books, please contact us at: **eduplayhub@gmail.com**

ISBN: 978-1091878839

Without your voice we don't exist.
Please, support us and leave a review!

Thank you!

This book belongs to:

Part I

Getting Ready

Start with training your child's hand control by tracing lines, straight and curve ones.

Coloring is welcome too!

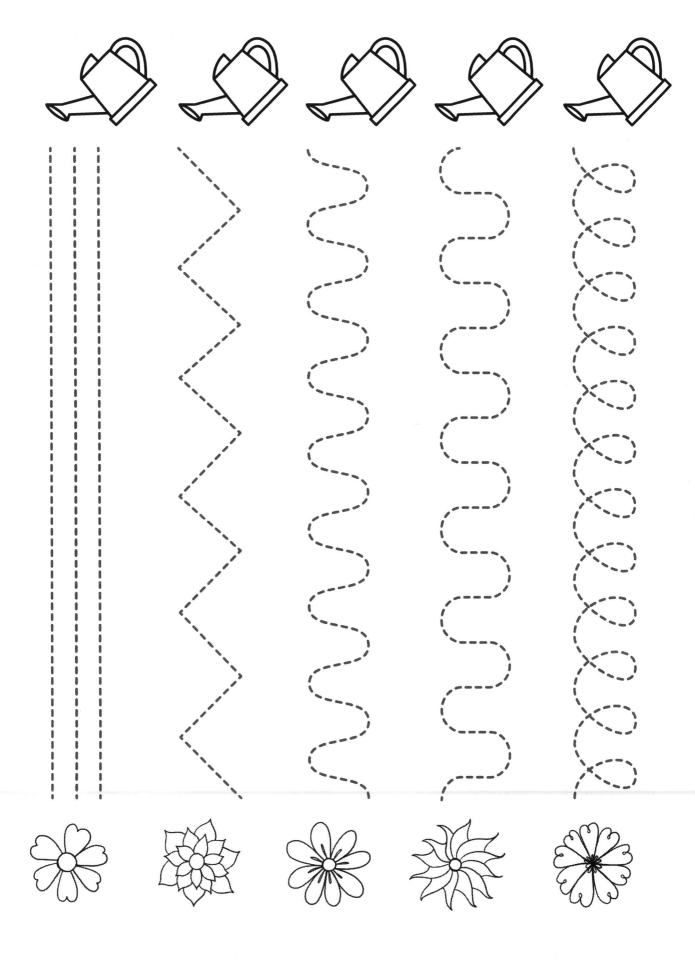

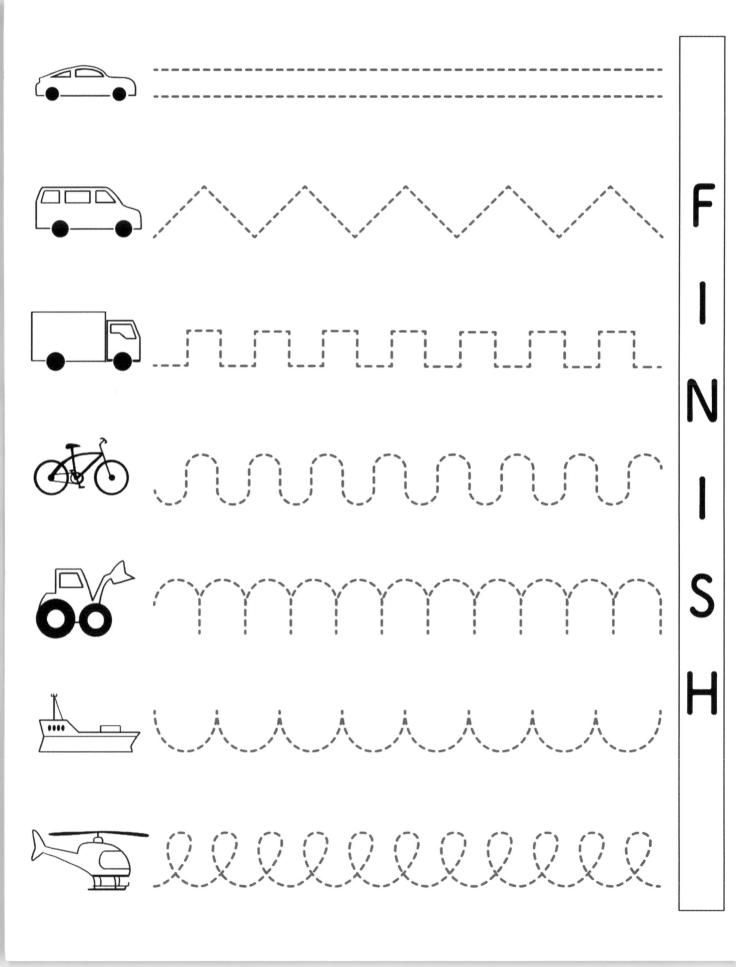

Part 2
Tracing Letters

Follow the lines to form the letters. Practice makes perfect.

Coloring is welcome too!

Adam   apple

A A A A A A A

A A A A A A A

A A A A A A A

a a a a a a a

a a a a a a a

a a a a a a a

Aa Aa Aa Aa Aa

books   Brielle

B B B B B B B

B B B B B B B

B B B B B B B

b b b b b b b

b b b b b b b

b b b b b b b

Bb Bb Bb Bb

Claire   cake

dog Daisy

D D D D D D D

D D D D D D D

D D D D D D D

d d d d d d d

d d d d d d d

d d d d d d d

Dd Dd Dd Dd

Eric   elephant

Faith   fish

George   gift

G G G G G G G

G G G G G G G

G G G G G G G

g g g g g g g

g g g g g g g

g g g g g g g

Gg Gg Gg Gg

heart   Hanna

Ian   ice cream

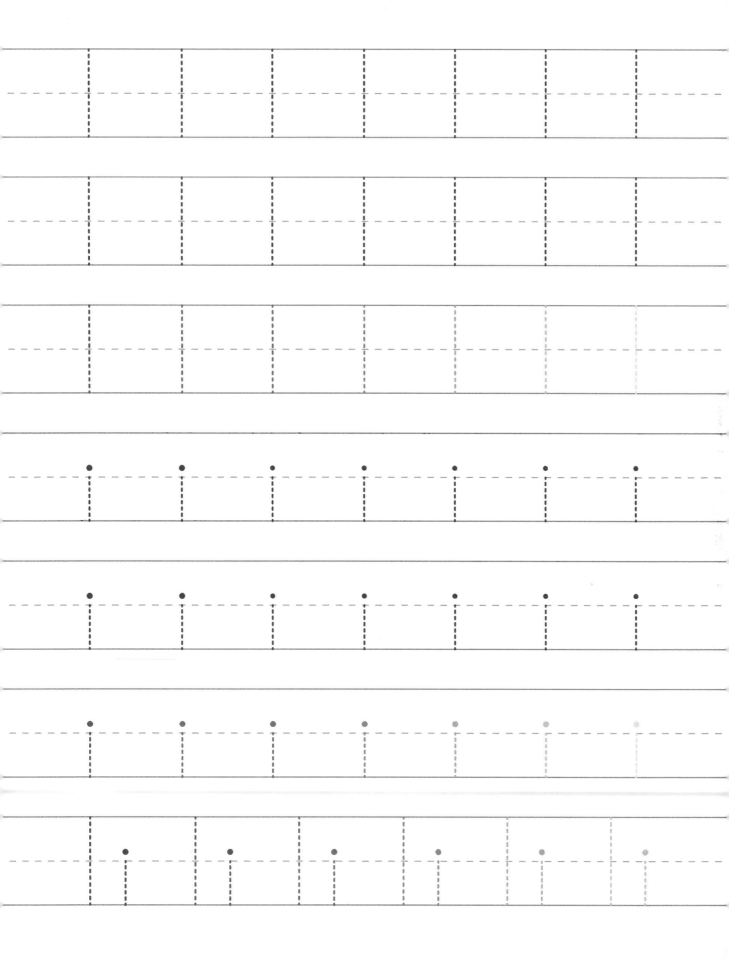

Jamie   juice

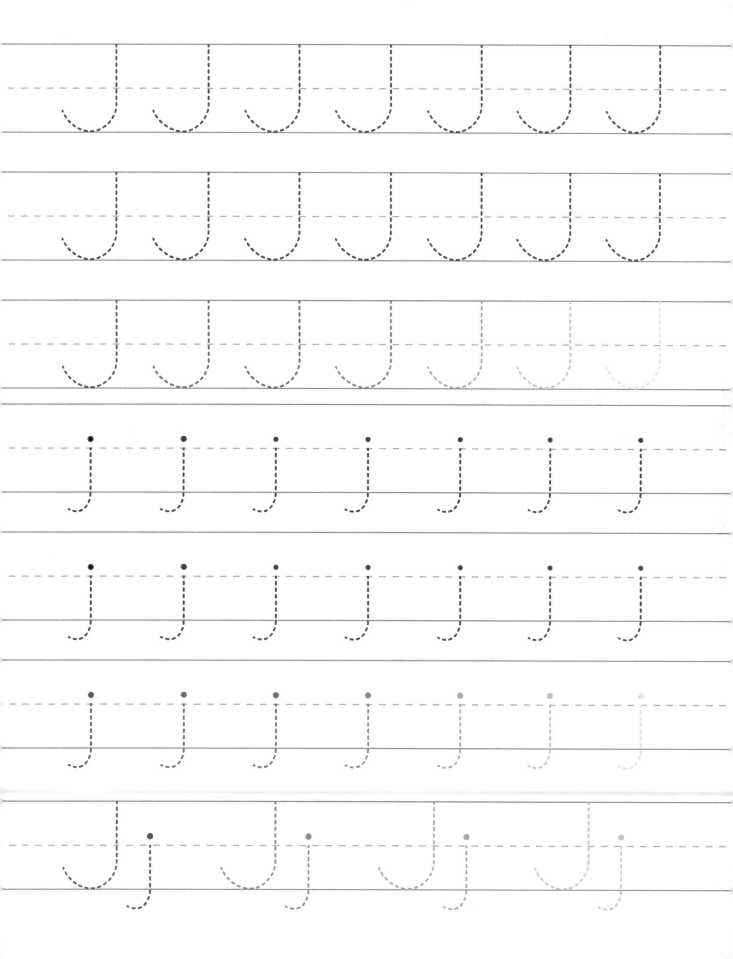

Kylie kite

Lily   ladybug

Molly monkey

MMMMMMM

MMMMMMM

MMMMMMM

mmmmmmm

mmmmmmm

mmmmmmm

Mm Mm Mm

Nick   notes

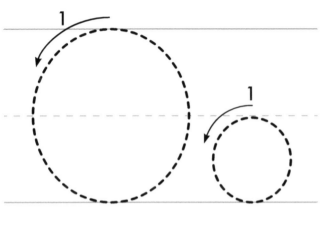

 Olivia

 onion

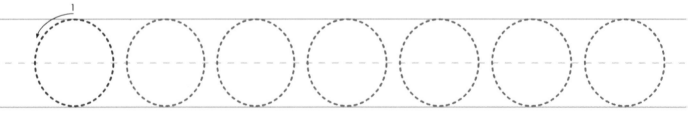

paint   Peter

P P P P P P P

P P P P P P P

P P P P P P P

p p p p p p p

p p p p p p p

p p p p p p p

Pp Pp Pp Pp Pp

Quentin question

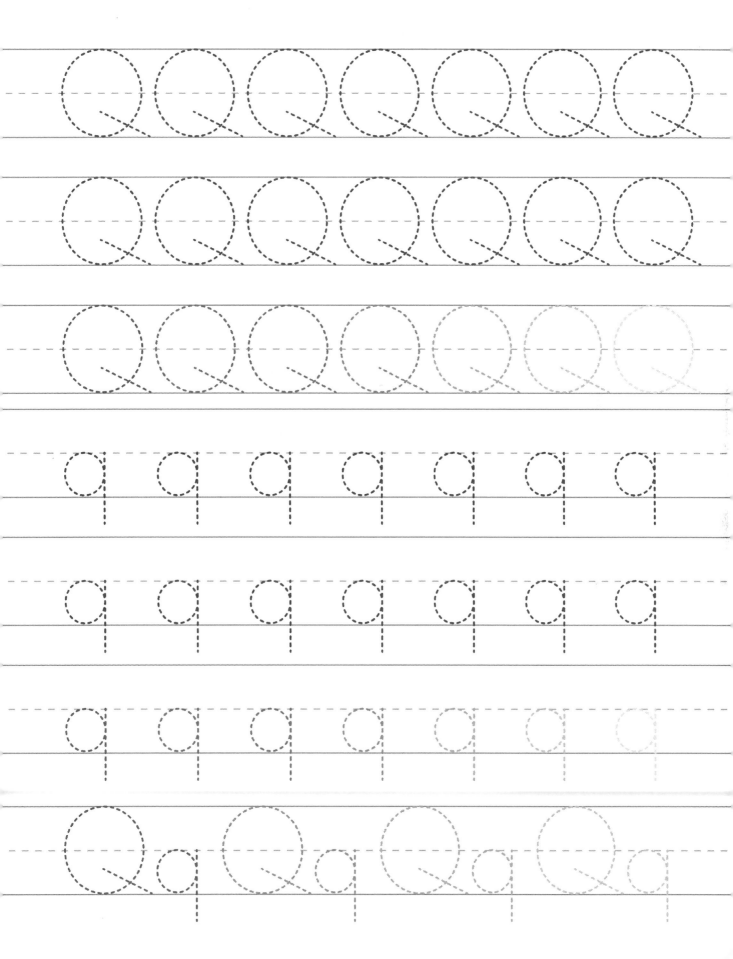

Rose   rose

R R R R R R R

R R R R R R R

R R R R R R R

r r r r r r r

r r r r r r r

r r r r r r r

Rr Rr Rr Rr Rr

Sam   star

S S S S S S

S S S S S S

S S S S S S

s s s s s s s

s s s s s s s

s s s s s s s

Ss Ss Ss Ss Ss

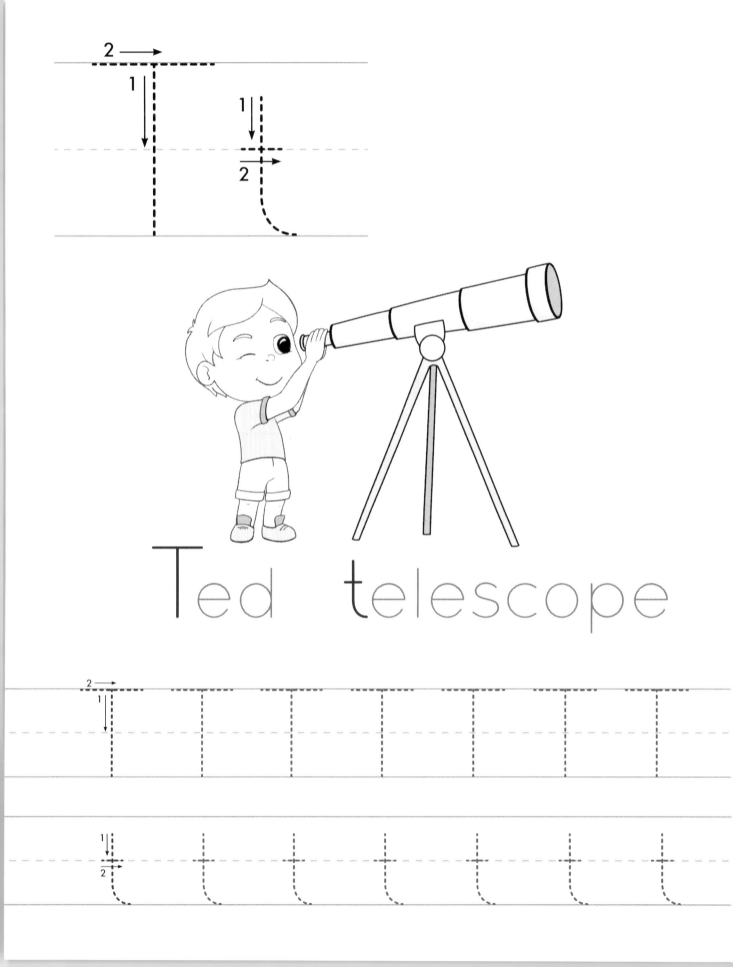

Ted telescope

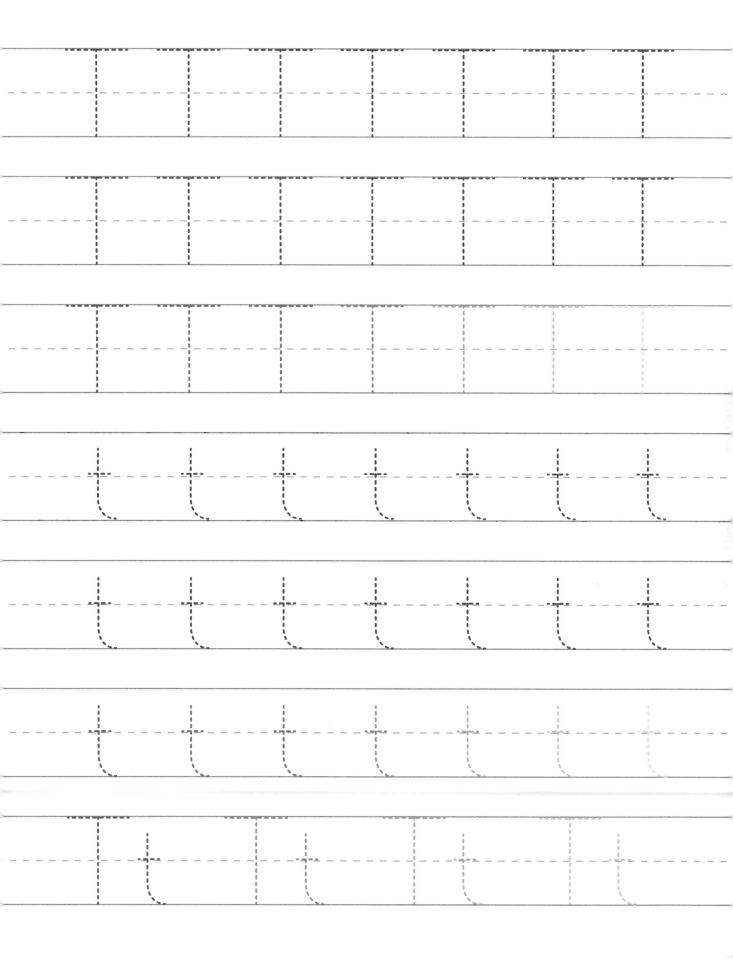

Uma   unicorn

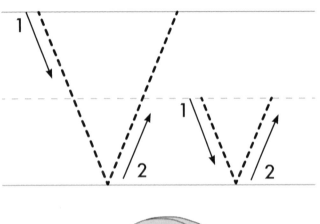

Violet

vase

Will   watermelon

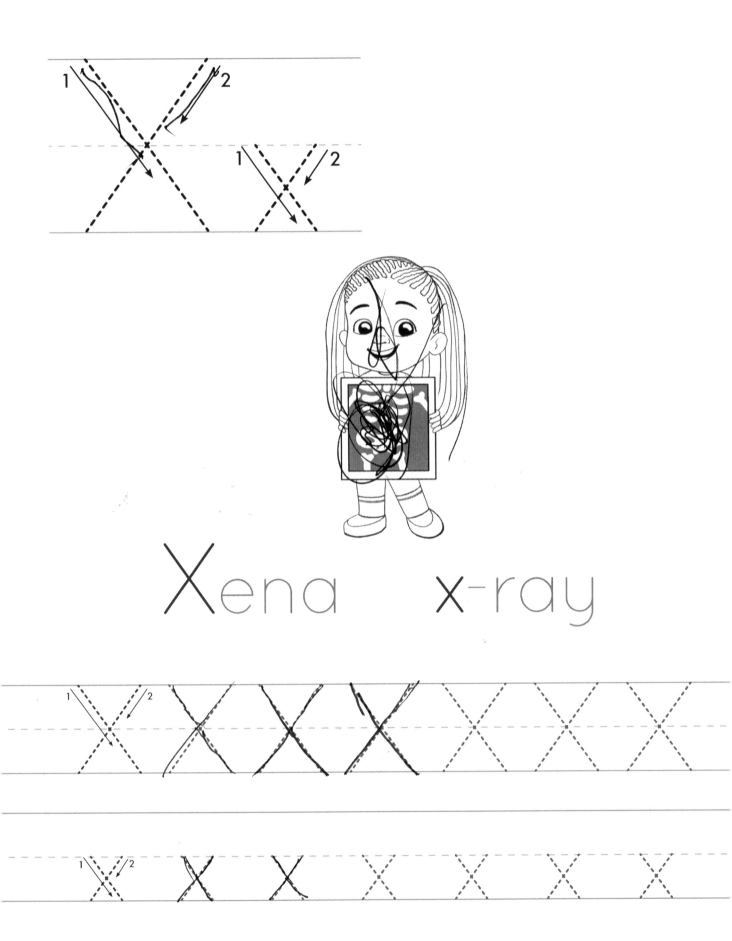

Xena   x-ray

yo-yo Yung

Zach

zipper

Part 3

Tracing Words

Keep practicing to master your writing skills while learning to recognize and form whole words.

apple

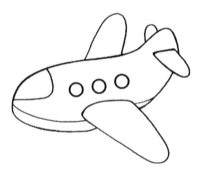

airplane

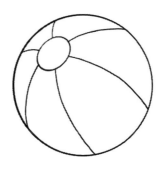

ball

books

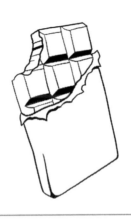

chocolate

cake

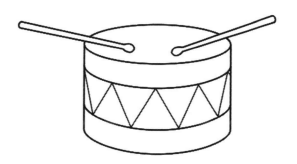

drum

dog

eyes

elephant

fish

flower

guitar

gift

heart

hat

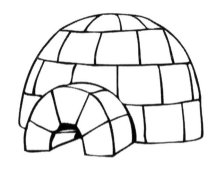

igloo

ice cream

jellyfish

juice

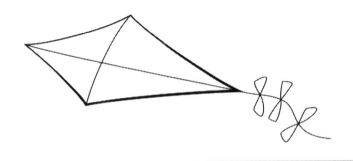

kite

key

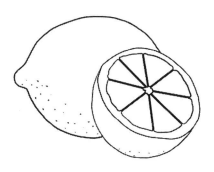

lemon

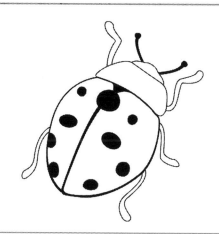

ladybug

mouse

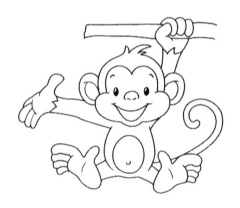

monkey

notes

nut

onion

owl

pizza

pencil

question

queen

rose

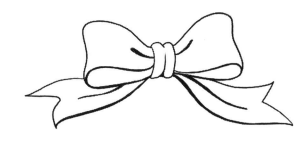

ribbon

star

shark

telephone

train

umbrella

unicorn

violet

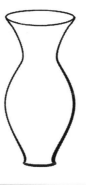

vase

watermelon

watch

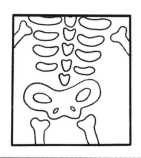

x-ray

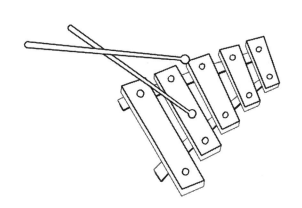

xylophone

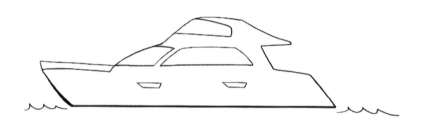

yacht

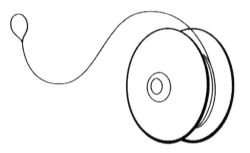

yo-yo

zebra

zipper

Part 4

Free Practice

Practice makes perfect. The next pages are
for free practice. Use them to write whatever
you want.

Hey there!

This letter tracing book is brought to you by Edu Play Hub. We believe that kids' early learning should be fun and challenging, not boring. Hopefully our books will help your child learn while having fun.

If you have any suggestion on how to improve this book, or what we can change or add to make it more useful particularly to you, please contact us.

Write us at:
eduplayhub@gmail.com

Or find us on our Facebook page:
facebook.com/eduplayhub

We would be more than happy to consider how to apply your suggestion to our next books and editions.

Thank you for buying ABC Letter Tracing for Preschoolers!

Please, support us and leave a review!

Thank you!
Edu Play Hub